This Ring of Stones
and Other Poems

ဆ

George Melvin Porter, DPhil

● ● ●

Illustrations by Ely Porter

All inquiries should be sent to:
Gallagher Close Publishing, LLC
214 Stratton Arlington Road, West Wardsboro, Vermont 05360
Printed in the United States of America

www.gallagherclosepublishing.com

ISBN: 978-1-7348283-4-4

First Edition 2024 (Paperback)

Contents

Contents

∙ ∙ ∙

ฒ

∙ ∙ ∙

Introduction

I have been writing poetry since I was very young. Fortunately, few of those early writings survived. During my turbulent adolescent years, writing became a passion. It became a way of dealing with the complexities of my own inner life, as Robert Frost seemed to have meant when he wrote that the writing of a poem 'ends in a clarification of life – not necessarily a great clarification, such as sects and cults are founded on, but in a momentary stay against confusion.'

Along with an ever-growing appreciation for the poetry of other artists and a love for words—for the sounds and combinations and visual impact, as well as significance and meaning—writing poetry has continued to be a way of finding my own momentary stays against confusion. Most of what I write, therefore, continues to be in first person, and many of the poems reflect this 'kicking at the darkness until it bleeds daylight' (Bruce Cockburn). Perhaps there's something autobiographical in all writing.

However, that doesn't mean I have had all the experiences I write about. That's not how writing works.

For a long time, my poetry did not see the light of day. Gradually, I became more open about letting others read some of my work, and these readers, in turn, wanted to read more. I began to publish a few pieces here and there.

Even while I write most often from my own need to write, and while some poems have been gifts for specific people, nevertheless, there is a connection to others. Over time, I have been repeatedly encouraged (not least by Nancy, my wife) to expand publishing my poetry.

I decided to put together a sort of 'sampler' of poems. They cover many years of writing, include many styles, and reflect those influences that have become part of who I am, in much the same way as when T. S. Elliot famously said, 'Good poets borrow, great poets steal.' He was talking about neither plagiarism nor imitation but rather about how the works of other artists become incorporated into the writer in a transformative way, not unlike how food eaten becomes a part of who we are. In a world of perhaps too many books and in which books have become easy to overlook, I struggled with why I should bring one more into being. In the end, I suppose, books are like people: there are perhaps too many in our world, and they are perhaps too easy to overlook, but each is, in so many ways, unique and each makes the world what it will be.

I started this project in 2015 while living in Thunder Bay, Ontario. I invited my son, Ely, a visual artist living in Vermont, to collaborate. He has contributed several original pieces and the cover drawing. Like writing itself, life has a way of interrupting plans, and this project has been 'on hold' for some time. During that time, I have moved and continued to write and have included two newer poems.

George Melvin Porter, DPhil
Southwick, Massachusetts

ഌ

This Ring of Stones
and Other Poems

ഌ

Dream of Oz

&

I dream of Oz
Of dancing in ruby slippers
Along the yellow brick road—
Of your uncomplicated kisses
Sparkling like emeralds
And your mask much bigger than your reality.
Can I make of you a metaphor?

For years
How long this waiting
For a life hidden in stone,
Unhewn and rough-cut,
Hidden deep in the rose heart
Of a grey, shapeless mass—
Cold granite
Hoping for the hands of Michelangelo.

&

● ● ●

● ● ●

The Storm

ℬ

Look upon heavy hanging winter skies
He is slow and cannot go a second mile—
Hear the fading sounds of the dying cries.

The weary look of death in his grey eyes,
The old man and his crew in the exile—
Look upon heavy hanging winter skies.

The storm rages against the night and tries
To kill the dream, and he must all the while—
Hear the fading sounds of the dying cries.

Along the coast of eternity dies
The hope of a lighthouse on a fog isle—
Look upon heavy hanging winter skies.

The fisherman will crash against the lies
Cast upon the beach with the ghost of a smile—
Hear the fading sounds of the dying cries.

A gull on liquid blue wings of day flies
Echoing the warnings of the night's trial—
Look upon heavy hanging winter skies!
Hear the fading sounds of the dying cries.

ℬ

• • •

• • •

Somewhere Out There

ဆ

Out there somewhere
Beyond the mist and fog
Lost in the fog and mist
Lies the sea
That drips on Aaron's salt-encrusted beard
To the tip of his chin-like cape.

I see you dancing like lovers on the face of God
Like angels on the head of a pin
And know that just as I will never join the ghost dancers of the aurora—
Those northern lights—
I will never join your music.

I am not a Maritimer
Nor shall I ever be one
But the sea belongs to me,
Or the sea doesn't belong to me—I belong to the sea.

I sit in the salt-sand of Herring Cove
examining memories I pull from my backpack
fingering, prodding the past
before I tuck it away like dreams that can never awaken
and know that when I die
my memories will die with my going.
Time is a cruel bitch and age her son.

ဆ

•   •   •

•   •   •

Seasons Change

&

Seasons change.
The apple blossoms don mourning colours
With a late frost
And spring greens hang shivering
In the air.
'Maybe we'll get together,'
we mumble
but our lives are too busy
and the bridges too fragile.

&

April 1985

• • •

• • •

The Eighth Sacrament
for Liz

₨

I cried the day you cut your hair.
Not that you were any less beautiful
But because I could no longer pretend
That the valley of the shadow of death
Was no more than biblical metaphor
Or a place I have never been before
Only seen on the rainbow-sundae map
In a long-ago public school classroom.

Nothing stops the perennial ocean surf
And nothing evades relentless time.
Shadows already stretch over the sand
Their only promise to grow still longer—
Does it matter whether slowly or quickly?

Yet into this time you and I will walk
In the unknown of your own lenten lands.
Through this mysterious, shifting landscape
Marked by sterile features, haunted by fear
Inhabited by white-robed angels
You and I will walk as friends will walk
And I will know as much as I am able
Of the sacrament of shared suffering.

The day you cut your hair, I cried.

₨

Herring Cove Beach, 02 May 2003

● ● ●

● ● ●

Leaving Havana

ଛଔ

It was raining flowers
The day I left Havana
A drifting rainbow of scented butterflies.
My spirit, matching the weather,
Was in turmoil
But not the turmoil of a storm at sea
More the quiet tumble of turquoise waves
On the white sands of Santa Maria del Mar
Or that distinct line of deep blue
Along the gulf stream
Where Hemingway's marlins lurk
Unseen like the mysteries of life.

Farewell, land of the palms,
The most beautiful place on earth—
Land of Martí and Che—
Homeland of many friends of my heart.

ଛଔ

José Martí International Airport, Havana, 2011

● ● ●

● ● ●

The Old Man in the Mirror

℘

Who does he see when I look at
The old man in the mirror?
Who does he see
The younger look of me?
I see the old man—
The old man sees me.

℘

• • •

• • •

When I Was Younger

&

When I was younger and thought myself old
I could taste variations in honey
And hear the slight movements of ruffled grouse
Creeping shyly through brittle autumn leaves
I could see wild light dancing on the snow
Or playing afternoon games on northern lakes.

&

● ● ●

● ● ●

This Ring of Stones
for Peter

&

When I am old, I'll come back to this place,
To this ring of stones,
And I'll remember other times we've spent
Together in other wilderness camps.

The stones will be blackened despite the years.
Trees will be taller, and fallen needles
Will blanket the ground like snow that first day.
Shrubs will push through the sand where our tent stood
And the fire-ashes will be cold and gone.
They will be nothing to those who pass by
Like our memories mean nothing to those
Who have not lived what we have lived.

And I'll walk again these lonely roads
Where, side by side, you and I stalked grouse.
I'll look deep into the dark mystery
Of lonely lakes where we fished
Look and see reflections of other days
And hear in quiet laughter of water
An echo of ours.

The ghosts of the past will walk in moonlight
Recalling other camps on other shores
Where cold and clear the whispering waters wake
And stir the mysterious meeting
Of light and darkness, a place at the edge—
At the very edge—where far away stars
And northern lights dance.

{Continued On Page 18}

{Continued From Page 17}

Snows of age will fall, gently whispering
Through the bare branches and green balsam bows
Slowly, quietly covering all sign
Of our passing—that we were ever here.

But this ring of stones will still remain
Like a blackened cairn of this time—our time—
And our friendship.

80

Montreal, Province of Quebec, 1998

To An Old Guide
for Bill Leschied

&

I saw your blue-grey eyes both clear and cold
Yet hot, too, alive and flaming, dancing
Across waters flashing gold and crimson
In the sunlight of that late summer day.
Spray stung my tender eyes until tears ran.
I groaned beneath a heavy portage load
I tangled lines
I hid knots, and you hid
Your laughter behind gruff faces and grey beard.

I know you have heard frigid ice blasting
Have seen the sun dancing with snow fairies
While hoary wolves cry out in lunar glow
And about loons you cannot even speak.
Something in their song, their crying laughter
Touches the place where your heart meets this land—
That indescribable place, haunted and loved.
They call it barren, call it desolate,
A waste, but they will never have your eyes.
What treasure you have in earthen vessels
They will never see, never touch the earth
Without gold-blinded hands and speed's crude power
Never know the gentle power waiting
To explode in dazzling, wild-light glory—
Just rocks and furs and board feet and headaches.

{Continued On Page 20}

{Continued From Page 19}

You told about some over-stuffed Yankee
Who would not pay you fifty lousy bucks
And complained the fish were small, the fire smoked,
And the ground was as hard and cold as life.

I wonder if you could find any rest
In anything but wool pants—the wool pants
You wore in spring, winter, summer, and fall
Whether in rain, sun, snow, or biting wind?
The lake brings waves to lap your wounded flesh
Cradling broken dreams in timeless age
Recalling the smoke of how many fires
In the silent nights of your memory.

ℰℭ

1982

Cape Breton Snapshot
for Erin

ନ୍ଦ

In the beginning—at the start of this adventure—
Time lay before us
Like a gift wrapped in bright colours
In hope and expectation
Dampened a bit by rain and cold
And by the half-hearted grumbling
Of the old man I have become.

But you brought me out past my years
For these few magical days
And drew forth the younger me
That still lives somewhere deep within
Folded beneath sheets of memories
Where I increasingly live my adventures.
You set me free to be in the moment—
To live, rather than just observe, life—
To bask in the luxury of now.

{Continued On Page 22}

{Continued From Page 21}

As smoke drifts from the cliff
Over the pounding surf of Meat Cove
I know at some point sometime somewhere
The end has come into view
And this time, too, will end—
The brilliant colours and wild cry of the sea—
Our shared solitude
Will fade into the sweet, subdued tones
Of remembering.

Yet I will have been changed
By this time—by you—
By touching together the untamed hand of God.

ഌ

Meat Cove, Cape Breton Island, Nova Scotia, 25 July 2011

The Call of the Magi

ဆ

West we went, south we traveled, and north
But east we dared not go.

The deserts we expected—wide and dry,
Punctuated by green sanctuaries
Nursed by the cool breasts of living water.

But who could foresee snow gilded mountains
And the borderlands, the places where wars start
Beyond which they say, 'There be dragons'
Those regions of fear—edge of the unknown—
Shadowlands of danger and excitement.

And at the end, an ordinary child
In whom lay hid mysteries—borderlands
Of spirit—shadowlands of the sacred.

ဆ

• • •

• • •

Of Weavers and Tapestries

'Almost anything that happens to us may be woven into the purposes of God.'
—Martin Luther King, Jr.

ဢ

Somehow in the tapestry of our lives
Unseen weavers of time have woven us
Together in the intricate patterns
We cannot see in final completeness.
Three unseen, though one visited the loom,
Work together in complex unity
The strands, broken and whole, coloured by life.
Even the very tangled webs
We ourselves have tried to fit for a nest
Are not discarded by the weavers' eyes;
They are included like gems of their love,
And faith, and power, that do not lose hope
When darkness and light clash in storms of pain.
Where we blindly try to pull on one strand,
Imagining that we have seen the whole,
The tapestry begins to unravel
And we must ask ourselves if the weavers
Have lied in the end or our impatience
Frustrated the pattern we cannot see.
Always the weavers start again to weave
What they can of what we have then undone
Until the tapestry is completed
Or until foolish ones toss it aside.

ဢ

November 1984

• • •

• • •

Sartre

ဢ

A man standing by the sea
Crying alone into the darkness
And the only voice comes of one
Drowning.

ဢ

• • •

• • •

Revenge Against the City

ॐ

Ha! In the morning
Quietly I shall walk
With only the sounds of stones—
Tranquility.

ॐ

10 October 1974

• • •

• • •

Lines Written upon Rereading *Birches*

ɞ

My father's farm boasts not many birches
And miles and miles from town I've had to learn
The simpler arts of solitary joy—
Friendship being a holiday treasure.
There in the late frost at the dusk of light,
Or naked in the burning sands of day,
The black widow of fear spun her grey web
Before my green lamb-eyes sightless in age.
In the spring dew at the dawn of summer,
Or naked in the crimson leaves of fall,
The hands of faceless time led me along
With the shapeless dreams of eternal suns
Down the twisted roads where stand darker trees
Not so easily tamed by ice storms.
So sparse were the birches along the way
That I have been the master of my oaks.

ɞ

Published in *In Broken Images*, 1976

• • •

• • •

O Frost

ॐ

O Frost, how did you block the winds of change
From blowing into lovers' quarrels?

O Frost, did you know ominous life-storms
That tear heart from soul, smother breath from life
And drown in great waves of helpless darkness
We who dwell near by lonely confusion
And the blue shadowed chaos of our fears?

How many of momentary stays will
I need know, if your example proves true?
How long are insanity's baying hounds
Kept at bay by feeble poetic flames
Echoing in empty nights of absence?

This bending of birches with ice—
Who can tell the frosting of hurt on joy
That threatens to twist and cripple the heart?
These ramblings do not sound of apples picked
Whether in care or by hands less gentle.
Who can speak of pain like growling hunger
That nags and haunts in low, grating voices
The very rest held for those who are loved
By a God who himself suffers these storms,
Who has chosen the paths less travelled by
And known the difference the choice has made,
Who has felt hot tears for ungathered joy
Rotting in desolate fields of our death?

{Continued On Page 34}

{Continued From Page 33}

But there the difference lies exposed, clear
Like gleaming snow on an unmended wall
And ringing bells of neighbourly strangeness:
He moved in a single way of service
I in solitude of selfish song.

ৰু

Merton's Bells

ℰℴ

I hear their crying.
It sounds like Merton's bells to me—
Like bells on a blue sky morning
Calling me to walk with you
Among your people
Calling me to walk as one of them
On behalf of you and
On behalf of them
Calling me to meet you face to face.

I hear their crying.
It sounds like Merton's bells to me—
Like bells on a blue sky morning
Calling me to walk with you
Among your people
As a shepherd
In the scattered flock of God.

I hear their crying—
Their dying pain.
It sounds like Merton's bells to me—
Like bells on any sky morning
When clouds allow no light.

{Continued On Page 36}

{Continued From Page 35}

I hear their crying
With tears falling one by one
Into some apocalyptic vial
Of your memory.
It sounds like Merton's bells to me.

I hear their silence.
It sounds like Merton's bells to me—
Calling me to walk among them
Among your people
Who can no longer cry.

I hear their laughter.
It sounds like Merton's bells to me.
I hear their anger.
And it sounds like Merton's bells.
I hear your people.
They sound like Merton's bells to me—
Calling me to come die and live
With you
Among your people.

ॐ

Mt Sinai House of Prayer, Winnipeg, 23 November 1986

Bonhoeffer

෨

I have read your book
But it is your life
That remains in my mind—
Disciple.

෨

• • •

• • •

To John

ℰℴ

The silent ringing
Of a haunted church bell
And the echo of old hymns
From an empty choir loft—

I saw you only once
But I knew you
To be a friend.

The wind blew into my eyes
And walked away.

ℰℴ

•   •   •

•   •   •

No Ducks in a Row?

෫ා

I do not have my ducks in a row.
They do not walk on the snow.
They do not walk on my toe.
They certainly do not walk in a row!

Some walk fast, some walk slow.
Some waddle-walk past
While others are on the go.
But none walk in a row!

I do not have my ducks in a row.
They do not walk that way
In a line, they will not stay.
Just why they won't, I can't say
But just the same, it really is so.
They will not stay in a row.
They will walk above or below.
They will not go where I tell them to go—
They will not grow because I tell them to grow!

I do not have my ducks in a row.
I do not keep them in a line.
They do not come when I call—
No, they do not come at all.
They cannot keep in step, I know
And I cannot tie their feet with twine.
I cannot keep them on the ball.

{Continued On Page 42}

{Continued From Page 41}

They waddle here, they waddle over there,
They waddle just about everywhere.
They waddle in a circle or in a square,
They almost seem to waddle nowhere.
But in a line they will not waddle anywhere!
Big ducks or ducks that are small
They just won't stay in line at all.
I do not have my ducks in a row—
That's a way they just will not go!

These ducks just will not stay in a row.
They seem to scatter where the winds blow.
Ducks in a line? It's just a country fable.
Queueing up these wild ducks of mine
Is a task beyond what I am able.
And they will not heed policeman nor read the sign.

Keeping ducks in a line must be a special knack.
Just listen to them quack!
I could stack them in a stack.
I could carry them in a black sack.
I could whack them on the back.
So cut me some slack—
And give me no more flack!

I do not have my ducks in a row—
In a row they just will not go!

℘

The Glacier Is Not Fast

ɛ)

The glacier is not fast—not even in terms of eternity.
Time has almost no meaning to the erosion
Worked in the secret depths of ice, sticks and stones
Power beyond perception, unseen force
Wearing down mountains and working away granite
Leaving behind sometimes broken and crushed rocky rubble
And sometimes sculptures of intricate beauty and detail.

And their hard and cold words,
Their icy looks and taunts,
What will they leave behind of your character
Your hopes and dreams?

ɛ)

• • •

• • •

So Many the Dead

ဢ

The dead—
So many the dead.
Behind the church
Are the oldest graves.
They laughed, they loved
They learned and read and cried,
But in the end they died.
And who knows you now
When time has scrubbed
Even your names and dates
From the black stones
Of remembrance?

ဢ

● ● ●

● ● ●

In Rows

&

Why are the dead always buried in rows
Their lichen-encrusted stones growing green
And yellow in the mists of passing days?
Is death such a frightening reality
That we must order its memory
To forget its pain and evade chaos?
We like to keep our dead in rows.

&

• • •

• • •

Funeral

&

There is no cry of triumph
No ringing bells and hymns of glory
In your dying time.

There are only weary faces
Shuffling feet, muffled coughs
And the softly spoken memories
We all carry
Toward our own dying.

&

Saco, Maine, 15 March 2000

• • •

• • •

In Passing

ฐา

Fall, having infested my soul with a melancholy
Love for the past, leaves unmourned in the early snow

Leaving me a slave to the unknown future—
A child of the past in a world of tomorrows.

And so, as light to shadow and night is passed,
The darkness of winter sleep waves ghostly hands

A signaling for the end of today's beginning
The end of all that is a half-dreamed dream.

ฐา

• • •

• • •

Father's Day Cards
Trilogy 2003

ℰↄ

1. Father's Day Cards

I see them everywhere
Father's Day cards
And they don't even know
You're dead.

2. More Father's Day Cards

I avoid them as long as I can.
I see so many Father's Day cards—
Rows and rows of them everywhere.
I want to push over these crowded shelves
To gather up these paper reminders
And throw them into the void you've left
That space where I miss your silly sayings
And the twinkle of mischief in your eyes.
They would fall around me like white petals
From the mountain laurel outside my window.

I know you would laugh at some of them
And, smiling through a promise of tears,
I hold one up, wondering if you see.

{Continued On Page 54}

{Continued From Page 53}

3. Last Father's Day Card

I miss you, Dad.
Whenever I walk again the places
Of my long-ago Wisconsin childhood
Every time I pull in the driveway
I expect to see your big grin and wave
Like Santa from a child's Christmas story.
Your absence aches
And the world is full
Of your absence.

℘

June 2003

Dover Beach Revisited

&

Two were we at the white shores of Dover
Timeless, with salt-spray stinging golden eyes.
Resting in eternal serenity,
You endure the ebb and flow of the tides.
Their uncertain seasons of rise and fall
Of conquest and defeat
On this lonely beach
Sculpt beauty as the silent word pleading:

The stable, the tree and the uncertain rock.

With what miracle of ease you find the peace
While I am borne in tempest and fury
Torn in the mythology of the moon
Holding sway this secret aquatic doom

Now drawn reluctantly toward sure rest
Now cast back, a frustrated fugitive.

I fled the inescapable pursuit,
Fighting the grasp of light and dying word
No longer silent in anguished combat,
Until the mad struggle is won at last.

Borne by warm prayers and cold drenchings
I am dragged as captive, defeated,
To the blood-stained shores of his victory—
A victory without question of loss.

&

• • •

• • •

Do You Think It Long
for Dorothy M.

ℰℛ

Do you think it long, this brief life of mine—
This eye wink between jests of time
With yesterday seeming so far away
Elusive tomorrow never coming?
Do you think seventy years a long time
To see that many wars and more tearing
The earth and its people from their birthright
Killing, wounding
Bleeding the holy heart
Taking no account of the divine image
Burning hidden in unaccounted lives?

How many years does it take singing songs
Of peace and justice, of hope in darkness
Mocking with black face in cold shadows
Among white-washed sepulchers, dim and raw,
Where mangled truth and stark lies are entombed?

Is it such a long time to stand between
White hate and black hate, white fear and black fear
While martyrs fall in bloodshot southern pools
And to stand with still new martyrs bleeding
Burning in Latin jungle villages
While Herodic clones massacre
A new wave of holy green innocents
In an open clinical holocaust?

{Continued On Page 58}

{Continued From Page 57}

The spring dance grew to midseason before
Young leaves began to fall prematurely
And the dance lost its step before its time
In wounds and tears, of suddenly broken
Dreams scattering through enveloping loss.

Is it a long time coming to this home
Finding divine spark in hollowness
And this family to dance a new dance
In these many arms of caring embrace?

&

1984

Basketball Church

ॐ

Screams and cheerleaders
Echo in the gym
Like a mountain river,
A voice of many waters,
But the Game
Is in another town—

Far away.

ॐ

• • •

• • •

Atheism

෪

For people like them
For people like you
Not
Like
Me

෪

• • •

• • •

As One Unknown

&

I didn't want my words to shed these tears.
I wanted to say sweet and happy things
Just to say the right thing—the perfect thing—
The thing that would draw you from summer's moon-spun dreams.

I wanted to kiss the flame of your smile
Lost in the wild song of your hair.

But I sat wrapped in silence
Clutching the tattered flag of my faith
Loving and fearing the tilted scales of justice.

And you, too, will remember me as one unknown.

&

• • •

• • •

Eddy

ℰℭ

How did it feel to be small and alone
When falling glass shattered in the vomit
Watching your mother, crying in her blood,
Tease strange lovers with hate-filled black eyes?
How did it feel to be hungry and cold
In the windowless home and crowded bed
When you saw their lewd faces drinking
And laughing joyless laughter in the night?

Did you tremble in the winter darkness
When the constable carried you away?

Did it feel warm in the house of strangers
Or did their pity leave you only cold
With your soul, like your infected body,
Unable to find its satisfaction?
How did it feel to be changing mothers
Like a used car nobody wants
Shifted from one unhappy hand to another
Without speaking a word to anyone?
How did it feel in the congested fear
Of your short life to number your mothers
And think of those real brothers and sisters
Living somewhere in other strangers' homes?

{Continued On Page 66}

{Continued From Page 65}

How did it feel learning to laugh and love
Torn between our own broken compassion
And cold, cruel politics of race and law?

Where will you go now, and what will you find?
How will it feel for a white-faced boy
To live with treaty numbers in his name
Or how will it feel to be Indian
Braiding raven feathers into blond hair?
Will you find a new way to call your own
Or will life bring an unanswered question
Rotting like unclaimed fruit beneath its tree?

ॐ

Let There Be Silence

ℬ

Let there be silence in a world
Torn by war
Raped by machines
Wracked by cries of pain
From the poor and children crushed by grinding
Politics and economics and sin.
The greed of our technological way
Our deep personal self-idolatry
Fills the stillness with empty promises
Like some cosmic political campaign
Ringing our ears with many hollow hopes.
Let there be silence in a world of noise
Endlessly echoing through confusion
And this mad rush that sweeps us helplessly
Along through incomprehensible life
Ignorant and fearful of the meaning
Of what is going on beyond our shells.

Let there be silence in the world to say
No to the sounds of powerful chaos
No to molding by principalities
And to sinister, sly shaping powers
Working in the dark, shadowy places
Unseen by mostly unsuspecting eyes
No to the stalking walk of death's angel.

{Continued On Page 68}

{Continued From Page 67}

Let there be silence in created earth
To feel the sting of rampant injustice
Burning white crosses in violent night
And bleeding wombs broken before new birth.

Let there be silence in a world of words
To hear the distant voice of God draw near
When saying no is not enough this time
When saying yes may not be as easy
As the clearly spoken refusal
To hold evil dear, instead of embracing
The stubbornly persisting Divine Yes
That will not return lost in darkness.

Let there be silence in the world to fall
And die, silence to await coming life,
Silence to become living parables.

Let there be silence in the world to touch
The crucified one around, among, and
With us as we move through the sacrament
Of incarnating his body and blood.

ॐ

1984

Sleeping Bear Song

ଛଠ

The winds are blowing harshly over them—
These desolate plains where buffalo fed
Before the mighty white sea in anthem
Flooded blood-rich hunting grounds of the dead.
The old people who walked in unison
With Earth Mother are joining her in dying,
Since traders and thieves with honey-sweet mouths
Have stolen away their buffalo gift.
How do they sleep, these sacred warriors
Slain by white papers from hot, burning pens?
Will more promises speak from rocky shores
While great chiefs lie asleep like infant wrens?
The voice of the wind echoes their cries
From days when shot and blood filled the skies.

ଛଠ

• • •

• • •

Twenty Four Hours

❧

There's an old man who lives in the park.
He sits in the dew of morning
Smiling as people hurry by

Smiling because,
While they all believe in morning,
He knows it's still yesterday.

❧

• • •

• • •

Infidel

ఓ

Enchanted I walk out beyond today
Down crystal frozen path and winding track
Parting in moonlight's broken silver dance.
My lone steps crunching in the soundless air
Crunching in the night's crisp frigidity
Through the snowbound whiteness and distances
Lying still before this green-edged blankness.

A long, hard going it was to avoid
Such hidden pots of slush, grey-feather blue
Beneath the unspeaking angelic white
Floundering through my mistaken choices
Until with warmer thoughts of far away
At last I face the ice wall keeping me
Out, or keeping them in
I wonder which.

Though it must be keeping me out I fear,
Since it is me struggling to break through
To hook below a wary northern trout
Thrashing at the final power of death,
The final movement of long, sleek shadows
In the winter-soul and brief daylight thaw.

{Continued On Page 74}

{Continued From Page 73}

I touch a fullness in the emptiness
So often mistaken for mystery.

When echoes of exploding ice have died
Away, and the chimes have grown still once more,
I feel the piercing cold and the silence
Like the heart searching for a word of God
And I turn looking away to the west
Taken up in the encompassing clouds
And blood-soaked eyes of the dying sun
An infidel of forsaken spaces.

❧

The Earth Must Cry

ॐ

The earth must cry, and too the land must sing
The dry blessings of autumnal leaf-fall
As crimson glory fades into decay,
Passing beyond the razor edge of time
Into frosted twilight of earth's seasons,
Scarlet flames in the sunset rays meted—
Extinguished and exhausted by living
Too long in spaces too short for growing.

The earth must cry the holy martyr's praise
The land must sing the mourner's lament of joy.
What for us the rise and fall of river's
Wild laughter on rocks and deadfall tangle?
No more how many the dancing fishes
In broken waters and white foaming breath?
How many songs in deadly awe silenced
Of loon and trumpeting swan gone beyond,
Of wind in needle and leaf and twig gone
Before killing rain and yellow caked mud?

Have you, too, seen the pines clinging to life
On balding rock faces, ledges and cracks
Too small and shallow for faithless courage?
We have broken sound and created light
We have violated the distant moon
And spewed unholy seed across the earth.

{Continued On Page 76}

{Continued From Page 75}

This land that nursed us from green days naked
And innocent, that weaned us in our youth
When we knew no better than to strut off
Like glutted cocks crowing our own praise.

This land tenderly calling in the last
Cold laughter of glacial mountain water
Desperately calling from bloated trout
And from the hoarse throats of black, choking loons
Ominously calling with the judgment:
By charred forest, by flood, and by dry eyes
Calling us to the wisdom of age.

I have seen ruffed grouse and ptarmigan
Left homeless in the land that once lay free
The whitetail starving and moose infested.
Ojibwa, Cree, Iroquois and the Sioux
Broken and dispossessed of their visions.
I have seen ravished children crying in
Numbers too big and too loud to be heard.
I have wept too, over one life broken
On jagged reef in an alcoholic sea
Corral built slowly from broken bottle
To broken bottle and over again
Too many one times more and now no more.

{Continued On Page 77}

{Continued From Page 76}

In the healing silence of distances
Too far removed from the hideous rush
For comfort of tourists and invaders,
With clowning loons dancing by sapphire day
And crying behind ruby-shadowed masks,
I have heard the piping calling to me.
In restless hours and in greening daydreams,
In chance vision, and in haunting smells,
In a movement of the wind, in the sun,
I have heard the sacred pipes of nature
No busyness of time nor style of life
Can wholly block beyond the tuned-heart ears.
I have heard whispers unvoiced in sunsets
And over the distance, the pipes calling.
Some will march to a different drummer
But I must follow the piping of Pan.

I must bear your bloodless, suffering cross
Haunted by the crying raven singing
An echo of your sacred song of death.

&

1983

• • •

• • •

Wine Dreams

ฬ

Play lonely songs and sad
Of shallow friendships
For someone caught
With spit in the soup
And blood in the tea.
Sing, music man, in a far distant memory of life
Straw grasping and gasping for breath.
Are you running from a law of life
Straight to the squalor of death,
A convict of empty verse?
They sang of homes
Down drinking their cheap wine.
Play on! Play on! Greek historian
Born under unfriendly eyes,
Born out of time,
Friends of what you have and not
Until the soul touches
And discovers the pain—
Alone again?
Where are those friends?
Ha! Fool!
Dream—yes, and dream again of friends riding alone,
Eating watermelons and grapes,
On a quiet old road
Beneath the Ontario sun.

{Continued On Page 80}

{Continued From Page 79}

Weeping fool, crying alone tonight
Under dirty city street lamps
Where tears are hidden in flight
Drinking the wine of a tramp.
Honour sacrificed to solitude
Are you dying godless and nude
In a gutter where nobody cares
But God?

ॐ

On Regal Bedside Throne You Sit As Queen

සා

On regal bedside throne you sit as queen
But he will know you when at last you come
Breaking with still hammer innocent green.

After so long the hours lying lean
While he hungers for table-fallen crumb
On regal bedside throne you sit as queen

Until your unholy hands reach unclean
Into the unviolated young slum
Breaking with still hammer innocent green.

Dreams have carried neither day nor night scene
Behind locked doors of guilty need, when dumb
On regal bedside throne you sit as queen.

What has come to pass enchains what has been
In empty visions of burning love's drum
Breaking with still hammer innocent green.

Thoughtless of what unseen stain will mean
Feeling the excited flame and spring plum
On regal bedside throne you sit as queen
Breaking with still hammer innocent green.

සා

• • •

• • •

Once I Thought
for Nancy

ಐ

Once I thought
That, because you are not
What I would have you to be,
I would—I could—remake you
In the image of...of what?
Some dream of something other?

Once I thought
That, because you are not
What I would have you to be,
I would refashion you
Into something I could love.

Once I thought
That, because I am not
What I would have me to be,
I would mold and shape you
To fit my need
The empty spaces
The shapelessness of my incompleteness.

{Continued On Page 84}

{Continued From Page 83}

But I see at times
the reflection—my reflection—
antique-tinted by the brown of your eyes—
one more changed by you.
And I am learning
like an infant totters in first faltering steps
because no thing can be loved
to love you as you are.

Once I thought
that you were not
what I would have you to be
but now I know
you are.

ॐ

14 February 1997

September 11

℘

Was September 11th really
The only day the world stopped turning?
Thousands died while I watched in disbelief
Thinking it must be a joke
A trailer for a new movie
Unable to grasp
That real people were really dying
Vaporised in black smoke and crushed.

That morning in September wasn't the only day
The world stopped turning.
Did it stop turning any less
On that night in January
Because it was only for me
That darkness fell—that my world ended
With falling dreams crushing my heart?

What will live again from these twisted ruins
Of the broken frame of our friendship
Is as unknown and uncertain as
What will rise from the ashes of New York.

℘

• • •

• • •

A Noble Company

෨

On a quiet night
I am all alone
With my thoughts

Dangerous.

෨

6 November 1974

• • •

• • •

Annsch

ଥ

Never forget, my friend,
The joy we shared
As tears fell in morning dew

Loneliness

ଥ

• • •

• • •

A Portrait of the Artist as a Man of Our Times

&

1.

You are like a man of our times, outwardly
Cold and steady—what you call only numb.
Anger seems the sole emotion I've seen
Strong enough to move your masculine calm
Mask, like long hands of time on Mt Rushmore.
What goes on behind those fixed ice-blue eyes?
Do you only use your anger, a tool
To safely hide those stubborn weaknesses
You aren't supposed to be able to feel?
Are you really as distant as you say
Or have you only just removed yourself?

2.

I've seen you standing alone and apart
From faceless crowds blending like cartoonish
Clones of sheep who have lost more than their tails.
You wear their clothes but are really a wolf.
Do you know that by thinking your own thoughts
Yet refusing to know your feeling heart
You also threaten to destroy yourself
To consume yourself like a bush burning
With the divinely hidden fire within?

{Continued On Page 92}

{Continued From Page 91}

You're like a man of our times, outwardly
Cold and steady—what you call only numb.
But today I saw through your angry mask.
I caught a glimpse of sorrow in your eyes
     And just a shadow of sadness as well.
You may still look like a man of our times
But wolf though you are, you will still lie down
     With the fetal green lamb you also are
In places only you will be strong enough
     To discover among living mountains
Where you are bound to roam as one free.

     I sat watching you create me anew
From brown lines and black shades, with your fingers
     Tracing my human form and bringing life
     Where there was only pencil and paper.

     At other times I watched you creating
     And breathing life into your own visions
Of the people and places, times and lives,
Of the way things are and yet ought to be.
     I listen to music you are making
I read short stories you are writing now
     And in watching, listening and reading
     I see you are like a man of our times
Outwardly cold, steady—what you call only numb
     But I also see the wolf roaming free
     With the shadow of a lamb in its tail—
     The shadow you try in vain to escape
That eludes capture to haunt your numbness.

{Continued On Page 93}

{Continued From Page 92}

3.

What does it mean for you to be an artist
And a man of our times at the same time?
Do you really believe you can live numb
And still paint or write or even make music
Still create the uncreated art
Still breathe life into lines and paper,
Oil and canvas, pen and ink, or steel strings?
What does it mean for you to be artist
And a man of our times at the same time?
How do you make love to a world you hate
And why give more life to a world dying?

What does it mean for a wolf like yourself
To be burdened with the heavy shadow
Of a lamb stubbornly refusing death
And just as stubbornly refusing birth?
Can you bear the bloodless cross of freedom
As a wolf suffering the adoration
Of the lamb dancing in the old garden
With new steps as timeless as the ancient
Around the forbidden tree of our times?

&

August and September 1984

• • •

• • •

Strangers and Friends

୫

Morning bells chiming from somewhere beyond
The unbroken stare of dull stained glass
Are calling me from dreams and memories.

In a few days you passed right by me
Barely a glance or trace of nervous smile.
In a few weeks you laughed along with me
And in a matter of time embraced me
As though singing to an unknown lover.

It has not been long to find joy and pain
In a heart of laughter and suffering.
We have shared our table and shared our sleep
And yet somehow our dreams have never touched.
We have travelled many miles together
But somehow our roads never really crossed.
We have smiled for the dawn sun and the lakes
We have laughed into the sunset country.
We have been greeted as kindred spirits.
Some have called us brothers of the green heart
And we would half believe that it was so
Knowing ourselves to be strangers and friends.

୫

• • •

• • •

The Ecstasy and the Agony

ဆ

1

We looked down, feigning friendly laughter
Like old friends chancing to meet on the way
To somewhere just this side of paradise
While the police, truncheons tapping against thighs,
Strolled past, looking at everyone.
You promised me two hits of ecstasy
But nabbed my twenty pounds and ran off
Down the dark and crowded streets of Soho.

2

I swam in the depths of your eyes—
O God, the ecstasy of your eyes!
We promised each other everything.
We would do so much and always be there
For each other and grow old together.
But in the end, you nicked my heart
And ran off down the dark alleys of time
Leaving me bleeding love through open
Wounded memories and broken dreams.

3

Sometimes love is more a savage ballet
Than a slow dance; sometimes love isn't pretty.
Beyond the veil of ordinariness
I taste unsatisfying satisfaction
And hear a shrill small voice calling to me
And I know what my future will hold:
I'll pick the pockets of eternity
And flee naked and laughing
Down the dark alleys of God's mind.

ဆ

• • •

• • •

To My Rapists

ဢ

Wasn't it enough for you to have my body—
To pierce my innocence with your lust?
Wasn't it enough for you to tear my naked youth—
To sear my spirit with your laughter?
Why did you have to steal my life?
Why did you have to break my spirit?

ဢ

• • •

• • •

Daydreaming a Different Youth

&

I close my eyes.
I'm young again,
Naked in the wind
With summer in my hair,
And I haven't wasted youth
Trapped in Siberian Wisconsin isolation
Or enchanted by adolescent insecurity and fear.

I laugh and risk living,
And live risking,
And indulge in a feast of freedom
Drunk on the careless wine:
Jeaux de vive.

I listen to tenor voices
I jive to rock and roll.

I love unashamed.

Looking into the eyes of my friend,
I believe I am loved there, too.

I don't hate myself.

I'm not ashamed.

&

• • •

• • •

A Theology of God in Auschwitz

℘

I am here waiting on God.

I was born long after the cattle cars
Stopped coming, bringing confused victims
Crammed into the gaping night of terror
The shame of nakedness and starvation
Long after the ovens grew cold and still
Long after black chimneys stopped smoking
And after false showers began to fall
Crumbling to dust among wild white flowers.

I was born in a world without Auschwitz—
A world with only the scar of Auschwitz—
Yet I know a secret we dare not speak:
In Auschwitz, the yellow Star of David
Met the pink triangle before the face
Of God's pain, awash with a lover's tears
On the twisted frame of a broken cross.

Here I am, waiting on God.
Here, I am waiting on God.

℘

North Truro, Massachusetts, 18 October 2003

• • •

• • •

The Other Camps

჻

When we speak of Auschwitz
Do we forget the other camps?

Maybe Auschwitz includes them
But they had names, too
And so did those who died there
And those few who survived.

჻

• • •

• • •

Icon of the Cross

&

The sun is melting in western skyline.
There's a hill under a rainbow out there
Where that boy died like some broken scarecrow
Tied fast to the post like a cross unseen

Or was it Jesus' undiscovered cross
Hidden beneath the accident of fence?

Could you dream of angels in black and white
Covering their faces with silver wings
Their bare feet dancing on cold, stony ground?
I hear wind moan like the breath of God
Crying from the out-stretched arms of the cross.

Did the same deep voice of suffering love
Whisper to you, Matthew, through the cold night
Holding your broken face with wounded hands?

I see tears like bleeding stars falling from
An eternal cross in the heart of God.

&

Hudson, Massachusetts, 12 October 2003

• • •

• • •

12 October

ℬ

I did nothing special to mark the day.
I didn't have to: I remember you.
Your death has coloured my life.
Your death has coloured the world.

ℬ

12 October 2002

• • •

• • •

Credo

&

In the movements of time and history
We who are orthodox conservatives—
Who fancy ourselves defenders of faith,
Guardians of divine truth and of God—
Are strangely reluctant to see truly
Slow to understand what God is saying
Reluctant to concede that we were wrong
That God is not boxed into our dogmas
God is not confined to our creeds or standards.
Gradually we've come to see that God
Is neither Jewish nor Gentile.
God never made some people to be slaves
Nor were some created to be masters.
God is no citizen of our own country.
God is both masculine and feminine.
We have admitted men and women
Both together are the image of God
Celebrate God's presence in sacrament
And shepherd wondering flocks of Jesus.
God doesn't favour right-handed people
Nor right-brained, nor right-winged either.
God does not despise the poor or outcast
God is not ashamed, neither of handicapped
Lame or mentally broken people.

{Continued On Page 112}

{Continued From Page 111}

God has neither abandoned nor cast off
Divorced people nor the suicidal.
We have gradually come to see that
Our God's colour is not for whites only
That God is Black, and God is Red, and God
Is all through the bold spectrum of races.
Isn't it time to look again boldly
And to realise that God is pink, too?
Isn't it time to realise that God
Means the rainbow promise for everyone?

෫ා

Provincetown, Massachusetts, 18 October 2003

A Lover's Quarrel with God

൚

The snow falls gently as I turn off lights
On this Christmas night
And know that one day not too far away
I will be turning them off one last time.
The fading angel will no longer flash
Yellow-and-blue atop my tinseled tree.

I'm old and have a lover's quarrel with God
Trying to find peace with my mortality.
In the silent night I seem only
To hear a restless call
To kick at the darkness
To rage against the dying of the light
Not going gentle into that good night.

൚

Fredericton, New Brunswick, 25 December 2011

• • •

• • •

A Wisconsin Christmas Carol

ℰℴ

'Will the circle be unbroken, by and by…?'
—Ada R. Havershon

The snow that began so gently
Quietly piles deep over the silent ground
Clinging to the spruce bows and oddly misplaced mulberry tree.

Do you sleep at peace in the soil
Of this Wisconsin farm
With which you had a lover's quarrel
For so many years?

We'll light up the house once more
And welcome the ghosts of Christmas past
As we gather around the table
To laugh and remember so many old stories.
The ghost of Christmas present will shape new ones
And the spirit of things that are not but might be
Will watch us from the unknown future.

Like all living things,
People die.
It's what they do.
But, in the sacred circle,
All dying things will live.

ℰℴ

• • •

• • •

Holding Lilly

ℬ

Your tiny sleeping face is the very
Incarnation of cherubic clichés—
A virtual icon of innocence—
And I put far away thoughts of passing years
Your growing years
When sweet green days are tried
By turning seasons: summer and autumn
And winter, cycles of decisions and
The brittle hurt of choices not yet made,
Preferring to linger in springtime's
Newness and curiousity in life
Without knowing hard borders, with all
Life and worlds full of possibilities,
Of adventures, all unknowing
Stinging insects that visit a flower
Blooming fresh in a world of grief and pain.
But I cannot push from me the awful,
Dreadful, pernicious realisation
That one day I will be a memory,
Vanishing like fast fading photographs,
A shadow someone you used to know
Who loved reading to you over and over
Who made hand-swings or tossed errant balls.
Will you know how much I have loved you
Preferring now to hold you still sleeping
Dreaming perhaps of the Big Yellow Duck
Of horses and splashing in mud puddles
Or tossing stones into clear mountain streams?

ℬ

Wardsboro, Vermont, 24 May 2016

• • •

• • •

Threnody for My Brother

℘

'Requiem aeternam dona eis, Domine'

Sometime,
In the after,
I will be able to think of you
Without hurting
And the memories that are everywhere
Will be sweet again.
But not now.

Someday the songs won't hurt.
But not today.

I see you in the dim light of the moon,
Rocking with the undulating water
Casting and reeling over and over
Tapping your foot to the beat of the oldies
Waiting for the splash
That would not only be a fish
But the fish.

{Continued On Page 120}

{Continued From Page 119}

A heron stands motionless
A loon cries
And for now, the raw slash of death
Bleeds into northern lakes
Cutting off memories
And there will be no more talking about everything
And about nothing
No more of whatever that was
We made by mixing wondering, laughing and silence.

Someday, in the after,
But not now.
Not yet.
Not today.

෨

Junction City, Wisconsin, 14 September 2019

• • •

• • •

• • •

• • •

About the Author: George Melvin Porter

George Melvin Porter has been writing poetry in a variety of styles since his youth. He has seen a number of poems printed in various publications, and has been a member of both the Society of Published Poets and the Wisconsin Society of Published Poets, as well as Diplomate Member of the Oxford Society of Scholars.

This is his first book-length publication, representing a sampling of poems drawn from different years and periods. Although a Canadian citizen, George currently lives in Southwick, Massachusetts, with his wife Nancy.

About the Illustrator: Ely 'El Gomoriso' Porter

Ely 'El Gomoriso' Porter is a self-taught artist primarily focusing on dark, surreal, and psychedelic illustrations in pen and ink. He is heavily influenced by music, philosophy, psychedelic culture, geometry, and esoteric languages and symbols (both sacred and profane). His signature is always done in the runes of J.R.R. Tolkien.

He was born in 1981 in Manitoba, Canada, and has been drawing since he could hold a pencil. Ely currently lives in Wardsboro, Vermont with his partner and their two children.

He has done album artwork, poetry illustrations, craft brew labels, private commissions and playing cards.

Ely's work can be found at www.ElyPorterArt.com as well as local art shows and private collections around the world.

က

This Ring of Stones
and Other Poems

က

www.ingramcontent.com/pod-product-compliance
Lightning Source LLC
LaVergne TN
LVHW051350080426
835509LV00020BA/3364